AFTER SUICIDE LOSS:

Coping with Your Grief

BOB BAUGHER, PH.D.

AND

JACK JORDAN, PH.D.

TABLE OF CONTENTS

First Printing: January, 2002
Second Printing: July, 2002
Third Printing: January, 2004

See last page for ordering multiple copies.

To the Reader

Someone you love or know -- a family member, a friend, a colleague at work -- has died from suicide.

This booklet was written to help you understand some of what you may experience during the next several months. It is not intended to tell you how to feel or what to do. You did not ask for this tragic event to take place in your life. You may be saying to yourself, "I don't want to read anything that will remind me of this event." We offer this information to help you cope with what may be the most traumatic event of your life. The material is arranged chronologically: common experiences during the first few days, weeks, and months, followed by the first full year and beyond. We close with Appendices which list valuable resources and other useful information.

We wrote this booklet with input from suicide survivors, the term commonly used for people who are surviving the death of a loved one to suicide. For now, surviving may seem like the hardest thing you've ever done in your life. We hope that what you are about to read will help.

THE FIRST FEW DAYS

This first section describes what you may be facing and feeling in the first few days after your loved one's death. If it has been more than a few days since the death, reading this sectipZˋmay not be necessary, although the information in it may still be valuable to you. Or you may want to skip to page 13: **The First Few Weeks.** If you do read this section, we offer a word of caution: Be careful not to criticize yourself for doing or not doing certain things. As you read the next few pages, you may catch yourself saying, "I should have done that." Or, "Why did I do that?" There is no "right" or "wrong" way to cope with such a catastrophic event. Instead, remind yourself that you did the best you could under extremely difficult circumstances.

Shock

Right now, you are likely in shock. Much of what has been happening does not seem real. People in shock say things such as:

"I can't believe this is happening."
"It seems like a bad dream -- a nightmare."
"I feel like I'm just going through the motions."
"I feel like I'm in a fog."
"Sometimes I forget what has happened."

Shock is a normal reaction to traumatic and overwhelming events. Your job right now is to take one thing at a time: and do what you need to do to get through each minute of each hour of each day. As time passes, you will begin to feel like the fog is clearing. This may take days, weeks, or months. When the fog starts to lift, you may find that the harsh, gut-wrenching reality is enveloping you. It hurts a lot. You may be thinking, "I can't survive this." Or, "I can't go on." This booklet will offer ways to help you and to seek help from others.

Witnessing the Suicide or Finding the Body

Perhaps you witnessed the suicide of your loved one. It is difficult to think of a more wrenching experience. The suicide may have followed an argument. Your loved one may have been intoxicated by alcohol or drugs. Or your loved one may have suffered from depression for a long time, or may have been despondent over a setback in life. On the other hand, your loved one may have given you absolutely no warning that he or she was thinking of suicide. You may have been the person to find your loved one's body, or perhaps you saw the body before it was taken away to the morgue.

If any of these things happened to you, then you may be experiencing not only grief but also emotional trauma. Images of your loved one's body, perhaps with frightening injuries, may be "burned" into your brain. In the days and weeks after the death, you may find yourself reliving this terrible experience. You may be suffering anxiety, confusion, anger, and disturbing physical sensations such as chest pains or breathing problems. These feelings and sensations may be accompanied by a strong sense of unreality, as if what happened was a nightmare from which you will soon wake up. You may feel as if you are outside your body, watching what is happening. You may also simply feel physically and emotionally numb, unable to register anything at all. Even if you did not actually witness the suicide or discover the body, you may still be having these reactions as you imagine the death scene over and over. All of these symptoms are normal trauma reactions that people may experience when confronted with a horrifying situation.

When people have been traumatized, they may also experience other distinct symptoms in reaction to the event. These can include intrusive memories or "flashbacks" of the scene, a strong fear about being re-exposed to another trauma, avoidance of reminders of the event, trouble sleeping or concentrating, and difficulty controlling physical or emotional responses. If you are experiencing these symptoms, understand that they are normal and that you are not "losing your mind." These responses will most likely fade as you recover from the shock of the suicide. If the trauma symptoms are disrupting your life, or if they persist for many weeks without diminishing, then it makes sense to seek help from a mental health professional trained to work with people who have been traumatized. Ask your primary care physician or member of the clergy for a referral to a professional who specializes in treating grief after a suicide, or contact a mental health clinic in your area to find such an individual.

The Hospital

If your loved one was taken to a hospital, there probably was very little in your control when you arrived. People made decisions without consulting you. Nurses, doctors, and staff people were quickly moving from patient to patient. Activity was swirling around you while you sat and waited, seemingly forever, for information. When the medical staff finally told you about your loved one, they may have been rushed or blunt in a way that added to your shock and distress. And even if you did not discover your loved one's body, you may have experienced a trauma reaction when you viewed the body in the hospital: shock, feelings of unreality, deep anger or fear, and other intense reactions indicating that your mind and your body were trying to make sense of something that did not make any sense at all. All of these experiences can make the shock of the suicide even more difficult to absorb. Sometimes after contact with the police or medical professionals, people berate themselves ("Why didn't I speak up?" or "Why did I let them treat me that way?"). Try not to be too hard on yourself -- you were in shock, and functioned to the best of your ability in a situation for which you were unprepared.

The People around You

Whether you are reading this booklet in the hospital, at home, or somewhere else, you deserve to have supportive people around you.

Ask yourself: "Whom do I want to have with me right now? Who can help me cope with this?" Then ask someone to find those people. This is a time when you need others to help you with everything: driving you around, taking your phone calls, helping with household chores, and just being by your side when you need to talk. Ask people directly: "Will you do this for me?" In addition, find someone who would be willing to keep friends and relatives informed of the latest information. You also have the right to ask someone to make sure that certain people will *not* be around you. Do what you feel is best for you.

The Investigation

Because suicide is considered an unnatural death, the police and local medical examiner or coroner must investigate it. Suicide is not a crime — but, unfortunately, homicides are sometimes made to look like suicides in order to cover real criminal activity. The police must treat the situation as a potential felony until they can establish that it was, in fact, a suicide. The police investigation begins when the first officers arrive on the scene of the death, and may continue for many days. Either before or after the funeral, the police will most likely want to meet with you. All of this can add to your distress and grief. While most police officers treat suicides with sensitivity, some do not. You should cooperate with the police in the investigation, but you (or a friend or relative) should ask them to conduct it as rapidly and sensitively as possible. Remember that neither you nor your loved one has committed a crime, and you do not deserve to be treated as if you had. If the police need to take certain items into their possession, please ask them to let you know what they are taking. We have heard too many stories of police confiscating items of tremendous emotional significance to the survivors (including suicide notes), without informing family members.

Viewing the Body of Your Loved One

The office of the medical examiner or coroner is responsible for conducting an autopsy in the case of a suicide, accident, homicide, or death of unknown cause. An autopsy is a surgical procedure performed on the body to determine the exact cause of death. In some cases, however, the autopsy report may not specify an exact cause. If you are the next of kin, you have a right to ask for the autopsy report, but be aware that you may not be allowed to obtain one until the investigation is complete.

One of the questions you may want to ask yourself is: "Do I wish to view the body?" Research with people who did choose to view the body indicates that most survivors later on feel they made the right decision. While they may forever carry that last image in their mind, they also feel that the experience helped them cope with the natural tendency to deny the reality of the death. Some people choose to view the body in the morgue (although this may not be an option), while other people wait to view it in the funeral home. If you decide to view the body, first call ahead to the morgue or funeral home to set up an appointment. Ask the following questions:

"What is the setting where I will view the body?"
"Will my loved one have any visible wounds?"
"Will you describe the condition of the body?"
"Will I be able to touch my loved one?"
"When will I be able to have the personal effects of my loved one?"
"What else should I know before I arrive?"

It is a good idea to bring a friend or relative with you so they can view the body or photographs first to determine if the sight might be too traumatic for you. In morgues and funeral homes, injured body parts are typically covered. If there are a large number of serious injuries, you may end up seeing only a small portion such as leg, hand or part of the face. The length of time your loved one will remain at the medical examiner's office varies from a day to several days, so call ahead to get an estimate. An autopsy must be performed before your loved one's body can be released to the funeral director.

The medical examiner's office may discourage you from viewing the body of your loved one if the suicide has caused significant damage, on the grounds that the sight will unduly upset you. This is a legitimate concern, but the decision about whether and how much of the body to view should be a decision for you to make. This is an extremely difficult moment for you, one that you will remember for the rest of your life. Take your time, and try to decide what will help you most in facing this situation.

Deciding What to Tell People

One difficult decision you face is how much to tell other people about the circumstances of the death. Although our society is slowly changing, there is still a tremendous amount of ignorance and stigma associated with suicide. Some survivors fear that others will blame the family or friends for the death, or assume that the family is "crazy." As a result, some survivors decide to keep the circumstances of death a secret. Within families, people sometimes try to hide the cause of death from others (particularly children), thinking it will protect those family members from a reality that is too difficult to bear, or believing that it may cause family members themselves to contemplate suicide.

While we cannot judge what is right for you, we can tell you that in the long run, most survivors are glad that they decided not to keep the facts a secret. Telling the truth has several advantages. It means that you do not have to keep track of who does and doesn't know about the situation. You do not have to waste emotional energy on pretending. You also do not need to worry about people (including children in your family) hearing about the suicide from an outsider.

Perhaps most important, if your family and friends know the truth, then they can truly offer comfort and support about what you are going through.

With most suicides, outsiders often already suspect that the death was self-inflicted. While undoubtedly some people will gossip or pass judgment about you and your family, most survivors are surprised at how accepting their friends and family are. They want to help, but don't know how. Some may admit, "I just don't know what to say." You can respond, "You just did -- you showed that you care enough to speak about it." You can help others to help you by sharing the truth and telling them what you need from them. For some survivors, just saying the word "suicide" is difficult. Today, many are steering away from the term "committed suicide" (because it sounds like committing a crime) in favor of "she died by suicide" or "he took his own life."

You may have some insight into the reasons for your loved one's suicide and may wish to share them with people who ask. On the other hand, your loved one's suicide may have come as a total shock. You may wonder, "But what do I tell people? I don't even understand this myself." Even if your loved one suffered from a psychiatric disorder and had been suicidal in the past, you are still probably struggling to make sense of the death. It's okay to share your confusion with others, perhaps saying something like, "I just don't understand this -- it's as senseless to me as it is to you." Over time, as you think it through over and over again, you may come to a better understanding of why your loved one took his or her life. Or perhaps, like many survivors, you will come to accept that you may never fully comprehend how your loved one could have done this.

Dealing with the Media

Depending upon the circumstances of the death, you and your family may be the subject of media attention. It's bad enough that your loved one has died -- now the TV, radio, newspaper, or even the Internet are involved. Many families of suicide victims say that the way the media treated them or reported the death compounded their grief.

Remember that you are under no obligation to speak to the media. Rather, you should think about whether there is something that the media can help you accomplish, such as publicly honoring your loved one or helping others to better understand suicide. One way to protect you and your family from being overwhelmed is to designate one spokesperson from the family to speak to the media. If you want, you can even choose to speak to just one reporter. If you feel comfortable with this media representative, you might agree to grant him or her exclusive rights to the story. While choosing one reporter and one family spokesperson may not sound like a satisfactory solution, most families who have tried this approach have found it useful. When other journalists call or appear on your doorstep (yes, it happens), you can dismiss them with the statement, "Our family spokesperson is talking with only one reporter and her name and phone number is _____." Or you can state that no one in your family is speaking to the media. This is always your right.

The Funeral or Memorial Service

Despite being in the depth of despair, most people want to have a funeral or memorial service for their loved one. Funerals allow everyone in the community who knew your loved one to pay respects, express grief, and comfort one another. Having some type of service will also allow you to confront the reality of the death and to receive much needed support from others. Despite this traumatic event, you must collect your thoughts and sort out the many tasks before you. Here is a list to help organize your thoughts about the funeral or memorial service:

Have I chosen a funeral home? If not, ask friends and relatives for a referral or look in the yellow pages of the phone book under "F".

Who can accompany me to arrange the funeral?

Do I want to compare costs between funeral homes?

Should a member of the clergy be contacted?

Who can notify family and friends?

Who can help make arrangements with people from out of town?

What tasks can be delegated?

Who can keep a record of cards, letters, and contributions?

What type of casket (wooden, metal, cloth-covered) do I want?

Prior to the funeral, do I want a private viewing of my loved one?

What clothing should I pick out for my loved one?

Will the service be religious or non-religious?

Do I want a funeral (body present) or memorial service (body absent)?

Is the church or funeral home large enough to handle the projected attendance?

For the funeral service do I want to order a picture video of my loved one's life? (Not all funeral homes offer this option.)

Do I want to arrange for somebody to videotape the service (for people who will not be present)?

Are there pictures or mementos I want to display at the funeral?

Who will conduct the service?

Are there friends or family members who want to participate in the funeral service?

Do people wish to write notes that will be placed in the casket?

What songs do I want or would my loved one have wanted?

Do I want flowers?

If people wish to make donations, what organization should they designate?

If there is a funeral, who should be the pallbearers?

Should there be a burial, cremation, or above ground entombment?

If there is to be a burial, what type of tombstone do I want?

What inscription should go on it?

If I want to put an obituary in the newspaper (which often costs more than $100), what should it say?

Who will deal with reporters if they arrive?

How will I pay for this?

Who can help write thank-you notes?

Keeping Organized

During the first week or so your home may be a constant blur of activity. People will be stopping by or calling to see if they can help in any way, offering their condolences and concerns. Consider asking someone to answer your phone and door for you. And remember that it's okay to tell people that you want some time alone. You may need to leave all the visitors in your living room and go lie down elsewhere. Do whatever nourishes your soul and brings you some measure of peace.

You may start thinking about which of your loved one's possessions to keep and which to give away. At this point postpone giving anything away. Almost all survivors appreciate the wisdom of this advice later on. You can read more about this in the section on **Deciding What to Keep**, on page 22.

During the funeral or memorial service, burial or cremation, you may appear to be calm and have everything under control. In reality, you are in shock. Later, you may remember very little of what has taken place (which can be a good reason to videotape the funeral). Time will seem to have stopped for you. You want the world to stop so you can let everybody know about your pain -- to let them know about the hole in your heart. You may want to shake the world and ask, "Don't you care? Look at what's happened!"

Unfortunately, you will soon probably realize that the world is not going to stop for you. In the midst of all your confusion it is important for you to find a way to organize the tasks that still need to be done. Many people find it helpful to make a list of things to do. Get a memo pad and, as things come to you, write everything down. Do not depend upon your memory.

Examples of what to write are:

A summary of each day's events during the first few weeks
    following the death
Memories of your loved one
People who called or visited.

Right now your life is a blur and writing will help you organize your thoughts and actions.

THE FIRST FEW WEEKS

Grief is a very individual thing. Each person's way of feeling and expressing loss is unique, and there is no single "correct" way to grieve. Here are some common reactions following a suicide loss:

Shock

Initially, shock is almost universal after a suicide. You may feel numb, dazed, and overwhelmed. Common signs of being in psychological shock include:

Problems in speaking
Disbelief
Feelings of unreality about the fact of the suicide
Feeling as if you were outside your body, living in a dream, and
    feeling so stunned that you seem to experience almost no
    emotions at all
Confusion and disorientation
Forgetfulness
Feeling as if you are in a fog or a dream
Trouble thinking clearly or focusing your attention

Problems in Concentration, Judgment, and Memory

Feeling distracted or absentminded
Difficulty in following conversations
Difficulty reading
Difficulty focusing on details
Problems in scheduling and remembering appointments
Problems remembering the location of keys and other daily items
Problems functioning at work
Inability to make decisions, even small ones; -- most experts
    suggest avoiding major decisions during the first year follow-
    ing a significant death.

Denial

Denial is natural in the beginning. The suicide may be too much to comprehend all at once. Here are some things that you might find yourself saying to yourself or to other people:

"No, it's not true!"
"This is a nightmare."
"I can't believe this!"
"This can't be happening to me"
"This could not have been a suicide"

Depression

A pattern of depressed mood and thinking are quite common soon after the suicide of a loved one. Some signs of being depressed are:

Feeling hopeless
Feeling that your life has no purpose
Crying, sometimes uncontrollably or at unexpected times
Inability to feel pleasure in anything
Finding it difficult to face each day
Lack of physical and emotional energy
Feeling like a terrible heaviness is pressing you down
A feeling of not wishing to go on with life
Profound sadness that is sometimes overwhelming

Fear

Fear is a common reaction to sudden death. You may be afraid of:

Going crazy -- losing your mind
Losing control
Another family member taking his or her life
Loving someone that much again
Seeing news reports of other tragedies
What people will say about your loved one, your family, or
    about you

The pain of grief suffered by other family members
People forgetting your loved one
Making mistakes that will endanger other people's safety or
    well being

Helplessness

One of the most difficult aspects of a suicide loss is the sense of helplessness it produces in survivors. You may have felt helpless to control the psychiatric, personal, or financial problems your loved one was experiencing. Perhaps you saw the suicide coming but were powerless to stop it. Perhaps your loved one resisted all of your attempts to help. Or perhaps you didn't see it coming at all. And now, you may feel helpless in coping with your grief. For the time being, just understand that almost all survivors have these feelings at one time or another -- and that there really are limits to how much anyone can do to prevent a suicide.

Anger

Survivors are sometimes surprised to realize how angry they are. Without your consent, your loved one has permanently changed your life. It is natural to feel angry. Here are some anger responses that you may experience:

Irritability and lack of patience
Feeling upset that your life has been ripped apart
Blaming others, yourself, or the person who died
Feeling angry that you will not share the future with your loved
    one
Feeling angry that your loved one could have been so indifferent
    to the impact of his or her death on your life.
Feeling resentful about not receiving the support you thought
    you would receive from others.
A strong physical urge to break or smash something
A need to scream, yell, or cry

Guilt/Responsibility

Whether or not you had anything to do with the death of your loved one, you may still believe you are guilty in some way. Feelings of guilt can be very strong in survivors. You may feel that you said or did something to trigger the suicide. Or you may believe that you neglected to do something that might have prevented the death. Either way, most survivors go through a long and sometimes difficult process of sorting out how much responsibility to take for the suicide and how much to let go. Try not to judge yourself with what one client called "the tyranny of hindsight." You can always find something that you might have done differently, based on what you know now. But at the time, you didn't know it or see it clearly. Try to remember this fact as you untangle the difficult questions of guilt around the suicide. Examples of guilt statements are:

"I did this." — "I'm to blame." —"It's my fault."
"If only I _____."
"I should have (or shouldn't have)_____."
"Why didn't I _____?"
"I should have seen it coming."

Rejection/Abandonment

One of the most painful aspects of suicide bereavement is the feeling that your loved one has deliberately chosen to leave you. This feels like outright rejection or abandonment. In most cases of suicide, the motives are much more complex, but to most survivors the death still feels personal and intentional. Survivors often think:

"How could she do this to me?"
"How could he leave our children?"
"What did I do to deserve this?"
"Why wasn't my love enough to keep him alive?"
"How could she leave me to cope all by myself?"
"I feel like he was trying to punish me

Physical Reactions

If any of these symptoms persist, you should be checked by a physician:

Loss of appetite
Sleep problems
Fatigue
Hyperactivity and physical restlessness -- a need to keep moving
    around
Loss of sexual interest
Nausea, diarrhea, or constipation
Dizziness
Shortness of breath
Headache
Chest pains
Any other persistent medical problem

Questioning

After a loved one's suicide, you may find yourself relentlessly asking questions:

"Why did this happen?"
"How did this happen?"
"What caused this?"
"Who is to blame?"
"What will happen now?"
"Will I always feel this way?"
"How can we go on?"

Relief

If the suicide was the endpoint of a long history of troubled behavior and mental suffering on the part of your loved one, you may find yourself feeling relief at the death. Just as when someone dies after a long and painful illness, it is natural to feel relief at the end of suffering. You may feel that your loved one has been freed of anguish, and you may feel relieved of the worry-filled struggle to help. If you have these feelings and thoughts, try not to judge yourself. Survivors often make the following statements:

"Things are calmer now without him."
"She felt so awful most of the time. At least she is at peace now."
"I used to worry all the time about whether he would kill himself."
"At least I don't have that to worry about anymore."
"In some ways, the holidays will be easier without having to
   worry about her."

Nightmares

Troubled dreams about the deceased, even nightmares, are common after a suicide. They are another sign of having been traumatized by the death.

Medication

If it hasn't happened already, you will likely be faced with the decision about whether to take medication to cope with the recent stressful events in your life. The two most common types of drugs used by bereaved people are those that reduce feelings of anxiety and those that reduce feelings of depression. Either of these might also help with sleep problems. Only you can decide whether or not to take medications. If you have further questions about this issue, call your physician and make an appointment to discuss whether a prescription drug will help you.

Reasons for taking prescription drugs: Medications can help a person cope with high levels of anxiety and depression following a traumatic death. Medication can help to level out the intense emotional responses, helping restore some sense of control and permitting the person to work on the tasks of daily living. These drugs can also reduce sleep problems. Many people who have taken medication for their grief report that it assisted them in getting through difficult times.

Reasons against taking prescription drugs: Most medications have side effects. Some anti-anxiety medications can be habit-forming, although this is not usually a problem if they are used as directed. Some antidepressant medications can have physical side effects that are distressing. Medications may sometimes make people feel out of touch with their own feelings and experience. Some survivors report that medications suppressed grief reactions that later needed to be addressed.

Whether or not you decide to use medication, understand that it is not a substitute for confronting your loss and working on the grief in your own way. If you have a history of psychological disorders (particularly depression), you may want to consider going on medications early in the bereavement process. On the other hand, if you have a history of substance abuse problems, you should talk with your physician about the advisability of using anti-anxiety medications, since these drugs can be habit-forming for people who are drinking or in recovery (the same is not true for antidepressant medications, which are not habit-forming). Do not accept medications from others; all prescription drugs should be used only under the supervision of a physician.

Gathering More Information

Some people want to find out as much as they can about the events surrounding the death of their loved one. Other people have no desire to do so. If you are in the first group, you may find that your investigation turns up information that comes as a surprise, even a shock. It is painful to realize that someone you loved and trusted hid parts of himself or herself from you. On the other hand, filling in the gaps may help you deal with the facts rather than blindly speculating about what happened. Factual knowledge gives you a foundation for making sense of an event that might otherwise remain incomprehensible.

However, your search for more information may also lead you down a series of blind alleys. This can be highly frustrating and add to the pain of your grief. We are not suggesting that you end your search for more facts. But try to prepare yourself in case your quest does not yield the results for which you were hoping. In rare cases, family members may disagree with the medical examiner or coroner's findings of suicide, convinced that the death was an accident or a homicide.

Trying to Make Sense

If you went through many years of watching your loved one struggle with suicidal thoughts and behaviors, then the death may not have been a complete surprise. This doesn't mean that you aren't feeling overwhelmed with grief, guilt, shame, and emotional pain. You may have thought your loved one was getting better. Or you knew that the suicide risk still existed, but you didn't know what else to do.

On the other hand the suicide may have been a total surprise. You did not see it coming and you ask over and over, "Why did this happen?" This intense questioning is one of the unique aspects of grief after suicide. People wish they could understand their loved ones' frame of mind and their motivation for ending their lives. Interviews with people who have survived their own suicide attempts reveal that a common motive for wanting to end life was the feeling that their intense, unremitting emotional pain would never cease. For these people, suicide was not so much a wish to be dead -- it was a desperate attempt to stop the pain.

Whether or not this was true for your loved one, it is likely that your questioning may continue for quite some time, although the intensity of the questioning should gradually diminish. Some survivors eventually feel that they do understand why their loved one died from suicide. Others come to accept that the suicide will remain an unsolvable mystery. Difficult as it may be, try not to blame yourself or others. With the benefit of hindsight, many survivors become aware of clues that they did not notice before the death. Survivors often say to themselves "If I had known he was going to do this, I would have done things differently." You must remember that, before the suicide, you probably could not have known that a suicide was imminent.

The Suicide Note

Sometimes people who end their life leave a note; but most do not. If your loved one left a note, you have probably read it over and over, looking for clues as to why he or she did this. Be aware that when people are acutely suicidal, they are almost always in an altered state of consciousness, and their thinking and emotions are not normal. For example, suicidal people sometimes believe that others will be better off without them. Or they see suicide as a way of getting revenge on someone else for a perceived emotional injury. Sometimes the note is just rambling and incoherent. In other words, the content of suicide notes can never fully explain why a person would choose to end his or her life.

When no note is left behind, survivors often wish there were some documentation of the deceased person's intent and final thoughts. Unfortunately, when people are acutely suicidal, they often are not thinking about those around them. Rather, they are focused on their pain, the problems they face, the hopelessness they feel, and the escape that they believe suicide will provide.

Deciding What to Keep

After a few weeks you may be in a position to give away a few of your loved one's possessions. We strongly suggest that you wait for at least a few months before making such decisions. During the first several weeks there may be items that you may be tempted to give away because you believe you have little use for them. Consider keeping them until more time has gone by. Remember, it is okay to wait. You do not have to do everything now. The possessions of loved ones carry a deep emotional significance, and the process of gradually deciding what to do with these items is an important part of the grieving process. For example, many people keep some of the clothing of their loved one, sometimes choosing to wear it or sleep with it for a while. A common statement is, "I keep his shirt because it still has his smell."

Life Goes on

Your sleep may be restless and you may wake up dreading having to face another day. Many of life's activities may seem meaningless. Even while you are faced with the constant reminder that your loved one has taken his or her life, you will be expected to go to work or school, pay bills, drive, eat, shower, run errands, and solve daily problems. You wonder how you can go on. But you do. And over time, daily demands can eventually help "pull" you back into life. Despite your tragic loss, life continues.

THE FIRST FEW MONTHS

The Grief Process

As the weeks and months go by, you may notice that shock and numbness have begun to diminish, and that you are more aware of what has happened and what is going on around you. At the same time you are also more aware of the pain of your grief. In suicide, guilt is a particularly troublesome grief reaction.

Guilt

As we have discussed, you may feel somehow responsible for the suicide. See if any of the following relate to you:*

Death-causation Guilt: You feel that you did something or failed to do something that led to the suicide.

Death-causation Guilt: You feel that you did something or failed to do something that led to the suicide.

"If-Only" Guilt: You say to yourself over and over, "If only I would have _____." Or "Why didn't I _____?"

Moral Guilt: You believe that you did something wrong months or years ago and you feel that this tragedy is somehow related to your wrongdoing.

Survival Guilt: You don't feel entitled to any happiness in your life. You feel guilty just for being alive, when your loved one suffered and died.

Grief Guilt: You feel that you are not grieving correctly.
Unmentionable Guilt—You feel guilty for reasons that you believe are too terrible to tell, or even let yourself think about.

"Getting Better" Guilt: You feel guilty for feeling better, and for having your life move on without your loved one.

---

* Several of these categories are found in an article by Miles, M.S. & Demi, A.S. (1986). Guilt in bereaved parents. In T. A. Rando [Ed], *Parental Loss of a Child.* Champaign, IL: Research Press Company.

There is no simple "fix" for the guilt that you may be feeling. But some facts may help you reevaluate your guilt. First, suicide is frequently associated with the presence of a psychiatric disorder, most often depression. People suffering from a severe psychiatric disorder are usually in a great deal of emotional turmoil and pain. As with physical illness, the severity of the pain intensifies the person's wish to find relief. Almost all suicides involve the powerful wish to find relief from emotional pain. It hurts to think of your loved one's emotional distress, but it is crucial to remember that there are limits to how much anyone can take away another person's distress. Just as no one can eliminate the grief that you feel right now, there were limits to what anyone could have done to fix your loved one's pain. This is particularly true if your loved one was convinced that suicide was the only source of relief. Of course, sometimes -- most frequently in adolescents -- suicide is the result of an unpredictable, impulsive act. Perhaps it is best to think of most suicides as an extreme choice. That choice was most likely born of suffering, desperation, and distorted thinking that may have been the result of some type of psychiatric disorder, but it was a decision nonetheless -- one for which you ultimately cannot be responsible. (For more on this, see Appendix B: **Suicide and Psychiatric Illness** on page 61.)

Second, once a person has decided to end his or her life, there are limits to how much anyone can do to stop the act. While many people who die from suicide are ambivalent about the decision, some are not. In fact, people sometimes find a way to kill themselves even when hospitalized on locked psychiatric units under careful supervision. In light of this fact, try to be realistic about how preventable the suicide was and how much you could have done to intervene. On some level, your loved one made a choice to end his or her suffering through suicide. We can wish with all our heart that our loved one would have chosen differently, but that choice was still his or hers to make.

Finally, even if you somehow feel that you did something that contributed to the suicide, or that you failed to prevent it, we encourage you to work towards self-forgiveness. Living through the suicide of a loved one confronts all survivors with a profound sense of their own limitations. These include the boundaries on our abilities to help others, to alleviate their suffering, or to predict or prevent a terrible thing from happening. They also include our own imperfections and mistakes. Both you and your loved one were, after all, only human. Your self-punishment will not erase past mistakes or bring your loved one back. You can perhaps best deal with your own guilt, and honor your loved one at the same time, by working to forgive yourself, your loved one, or whomever you hold responsible for the death, and by trying to become a better person as a result of this tragedy.

If the Death is a Challenge to Your Faith

The suicide of your loved one may challenge your religion or your spiritual beliefs. Suicide also raises deep questions for some people about why God could allow suicide to even exist in the world. Historically, many religions have condemned suicide and sometimes even the family survivors. Today, however, most religious groups recognize that suicide is usually the result of a psychiatric disorder, and take a more compassionate view. These are important issues that you, like many other people, may need to sort out for yourself. Consider talking to a clergyperson, a therapist, or perhaps a friend who seems to have a compassionate and spiritual approach to life. In addition, try also to find someone who has factual knowledge about suicide and the conditions that contribute to it.

Your Family in Grief

Suicide can pull apart the fabric of a family. Each family member's way of coping is unique. Men often grieve differently than women, and children grieve differently than adults. Family members may have a hard time communicating because they are each immersed in their own pain. Some may feel the suicide has brought shame upon themselves and the family. They may blame one another for not doing more to prevent the death. Teenagers (and adults) may feel that everyone is looking at them. They may have problems dealing with the flood of emotions they are experiencing. At the end of this booklet, you will find resources for getting help. As much as you can, be there for the children in your family and keep the lines of communication open. Talk together about what has happened and what it means to each person in the family. Try to do this without judging one another's feelings or manner of grieving, unless the person's way of coping is dangerous or causing harm.

While no family member will be exempt from grieving the suicide of a loved one, the actual displays of grief will run the entire range of emotions. Some people openly express their sadness, whereas others may show little or no sorrow. Never measure a person's grief by tears or lack of tears. How a person grieves depends on many factors: personality, previous experiences with loss, one's relationship with the person who died, and what a person thinks that others expect. Many who try to avoid talking about and feeling the reality of a traumatic death later say, "It was even more difficult to deal with it later on." While some adults and children in your life may seem as though they are not grieving and are unemotional, keep in mind that you cannot make a person grieve.

Sometimes survivors feel that it is best not to bring up the painful topic of the death, because it will upset others in the family. Sometimes this is true, but remember that shared silence does not always mean everyone is coping well. Having something on your mind without being able to discuss it is usually more difficult than talking about it with a good listener. It is okay to ask family members, "Do you feel like talking about it?" and let the individual decide if now is the time to open up.

Denial and silence may seem helpful in quelling the pain of the loss -- for a while. At first, many people try not to think about the death, the pain, and the dreadful reality that their loved one is never going to return. Eventually you will be faced with numerous reminders that this event really did take place. For some survivors, the reality of the tragedy may register within a few weeks following the death. For others, it takes several months, even a year or more before it really sinks in.

The healthiest path for most people seems to involve learning to "dose" yourself, balancing the times when you confront the loss and those when you avoid it. Learn to talk about the death and your relationship with the deceased with a trusted, non-judgmental family member or friend. Do this regularly, even if you would rather avoid the topic altogether. When you need a break, it is okay to distract yourself with healthy ways of taking your mind off your grief. These might include watching television, listening to uplifting music, visiting the Internet, going shopping, working on a hobby, or visiting a new place. By learning to confront your loss a little bit at a time, you will develop skills for coping with it. Eventually it will become more manageable.

Continuing Bonds

Unlike most other cultures, our society expects grief to be a relatively short-term experience: You may encounter advice such as "Get over it and get on with your life." "Don't dwell on the past." "What's done is done." Many people expect you to quickly reach "closure," as if the tragedy was an unfortunate but finite event that you should put behind you.

In fact, however, most suicide survivors find that they never arrive at a point in their loss where they can say, "Now it's all over with." While your life goes on, your loved one remains gone. Your task is to learn to live with this permanent change in your life, not to get over a temporary disruption. If you are like most people, with time and support you will be able to integrate this change into your life. For many survivors, this means forging a new kind of connection to their loved one, a continuing bond of love. There are many ways to do this. Talking about your loved one with others, talking to your loved one directly (yes, this is normal), participating in rituals that honor or memorialize the deceased -- almost any activity that helps you to maintain your sense of connection to your loved one is fine, as long as you are not using it to pretend he or she is still physically alive, and as long as it does not prevent you from gradually reinvesting in life. Some survivors say that instead of trying to maintain their old, normal life, they learn to find a "different normal." You are suffering from a broken heart and your soul has been wounded. You will never forget your loved one. The pain of loss will soften and diminish, but the love you shared is yours to keep for the rest of your life.

Children and Grief

Children can only grieve at their own level of maturity. Depending on their age and maturity level, they may have difficulty understanding what death means. Young children usually do not understand that death is a permanent, irreversible condition, and that the loved one's body has stopped working completely. They may ask why the loved one cannot come back to life. Or they may worry about how the deceased will find food or water. Be patient with these questions, since they reflect a developmental inability to grasp the meaning of biological death. Try to give simple, honest answers to your children's questions, and take your lead from their responses. Children do mourn, but they may show their grief differently than adults. These ways reflect the level at which your child is presently able to come to terms with death. Their understanding will change as they develop through the years.

We want to address again the important question of whether to tell your children the truth about the circumstances of the death. In an attempt to protect children, well-meaning adults may consider not revealing that the death was a suicide. But even if children do not know the facts of a situation, they are usually keenly aware of the emotional responses of the adults around them. They know something very upsetting has happened, and without knowing the facts, they will tend to construct their own (often incorrect) explanation, sometimes blaming themselves. Many parents are also surprised to find how much their children are worried about their parent's well being after the loss, particularly if it was the other parent who died from suicide.

Maintaining silence or lying about the cause of death teaches children that some things are so awful they just cannot be talked about. At times, you may feel this way yourself about the suicide. But silence and deception leaves children feeling alone, confused, and too ashamed or frightened to talk about what's on their mind. There is enough pain for everyone in your family right now, and communicating honestly about the suicide allows family members -- including children -- to support one another.

Finally, it is worth repeating that eventually your child will probably figure out what happened, or else hear it from someone else. When children or adults discover months or years later that a death was a suicide, they have the additional distress of absorbing information that they realize should have been given to them from the start. For this reason, it is almost always better for a child to learn the truth from you at or near the time of the death. You can decide how many of the details to divulge by gauging your child's reactions and listening to the questions he or she asks. Most child therapists agree that it's important for the child to understand that the individual died through suicide. Your child can make better sense of this brutal fact with the help of a trusted adult. If you need help with this difficult task, seek a consultation from an experienced child therapist.

Once you sit down and tell your child, be silent and listen for questions. Answer truthfully. If the child asks, "Why did _____ kill himself or herself?" you might reply, "I'm not sure myself." If you feel that you do understand the reasons behind the death, try to convey them in terms appropriate to the maturity level of your child. For example, you might say something like, "Daddy had an illness that made him feel very, very sad and discouraged. That illness is called depression. His depression got so bad that he did not feel that he could go on living anymore." Depending on how close the child was to your loved one, and on your child's particular coping style, you may or may not notice a distinct change in the child's behavior. Infants and preschoolers may become more whiny and unruly. School age children may show increased behavior problems at home and at school. Treat these difficulties as you normally would, but be willing to accept that the behavior is probably a temporary reaction to the death. Just as you are not yourself right now but will eventually find your equilibrium again, with support and patience your children will do likewise.

Guilt in Children

When a death occurs, especially a suicide, children are highly susceptible to guilt. Consider sitting down with your child within a few weeks after the suicide and state the following as a way to tap into that guilt: "Sometimes when someone dies, we may think that it is due to something we said or did -- did you ever feel that way about _____'s death?" Follow this question with silence. This will permit your child to think about what you said and perhaps respond with an honest answer. If your child denies feeling this way, reinforce that healthy denial by saying, "Good, I'm glad to hear that. I want you to know that it is never a child's fault when a grown-up ends his or her life. In fact, _____'s death was no one's fault." If the child does feel guilty, gently explain that while guilt feelings are normal, the child's actions did not cause the suicide. You may also want to acknowledge that you have similar feelings sometimes and share some of the ways that you are coping with these emotions. Encourage your child to speak with you about this issue at any time, and follow up the conversation with "check-ins" to see how your child is confronting guilt as time goes by.

(Re)Visiting the Scene

If the suicide took place somewhere other than in your home, you may have thought about visiting the scene. Some people have no desire to visit or revisit the place where their loved one died. Other people have mixed feelings about visiting the scene, while others have decided that they are definitely going. If you are considering a visit, answer the following questions for yourself first:

What are my present emotional reactions when I think about going there?

Who should I take with me for support?

What do I expect to happen once I get there?

Once I visit the scene, how can I take care of myself so that I will be okay?

Some people who visit the scene consider finding a way that the place can be preserved or commemorated in memory of their loved one. Be aware that whatever you do may not be permanent. You may leave something at the scene, for example, only to later find it has been removed.

Flashbacks

A common reaction following a tragic death is a replaying of the event—or the event as you imagined it -- over and over in your head. We mentioned this earlier in the section on **Witnessing the Suicide** (page 3). This flashback response may or may not feel under your control. It may interfere with your ability to concentrate and carry out daily activities. One of the most frequent recurring thoughts is, "What was my loved one thinking and feeling during this time?"

Survivors typically replay what they imagine the scene was in the last few moments of their loved one's life. Your reactions to this scene may include sorrow over how much pain your loved one was in, regret that you were not able to save your loved one or to say good-bye, and great distress over the horror of the event.

If you continue to have disruptive thoughts, you may wish to try a technique called "thought-stopping." Whenever you begin to have intrusive thoughts, say to yourself, loudly and firmly, "STOP!" Doing this can diminish the thoughts and images that interfere with your daily tasks. If these thoughts continue to be a problem, contact an experienced mental health professional who can work with you. There are additional techniques that can be effective in controlling these intrusive flashbacks.

Reactions of Other People and Feeling Stigmatized

Unfortunately, after a suicide, you and your family members may feel negatively judged by others. Whether intentional or not, some people ask questions and say things that suggest blame, neglect, or some failure on your part. People may also be awkward in their attempts to offer support. Up to a point, try to bear with people who say or do insensitive things -- but also think about how you want to end the discussion if they do not stop. Sometimes, even you may feel that the suicide reflects poorly on your family. Implied criticism and blame from others may lead you to pull away from your social network and decide that only a few select people (such as other suicide survivors) can grasp your experience.

You may feel uncertain about how to act and what exactly to share with others. You may find that, like you, people are trying to make sense of the death. They may expect you to be able to give an explanation for something that may still be very confusing to you. Or they may say things that reflect common misconceptions about suicide in our society ("Something must have driven him to it." "She must have been crazy." "I thought only teenagers killed themselves."). People may feel it is appropriate to show their anger toward your loved one, which may cause you even more pain. To head off these comments, you will often need to be assertive, telling others what they can do to be of help. For example, you may want to say, "It's okay to bring up Jim's name -- it helps me to talk about him." Conversely, sometimes you may need to say, "I need a break. Let's not talk about Jim or how I'm doing right now." And you always have the right to say, "I just can't answer that question right now".

Even people who were initially supportive and surrounded you during the immediate crisis may leave you and return to their families and their respective lives. As time goes by, some of the people who attended the funeral may not show up again. They may not understand how permanently altered your life is, and may simply expect you to get back to your old self. When your friends find out that the old you is gone, some will remain steadfast, but others will slip quietly out of your life.

Though most people want to support you through this difficult time, they may not know what to say or do that will be of help. It is crucial that you learn to avoid people who offer simplistic explanations or painful moral judgments about the suicide. As you regain strength, you may choose to educate people who misunderstand suicide. But it is equally important that you seek out those who genuinely do want to help, even though they sometimes feel as helpless as you do. Over time, you will learn what it is that others can do to offer support, and you can explain to your friends and family how to respond more compassionately. Sometimes all you need is a friend to sit beside you and hold your hand. Sometimes, there are simply no words. Also, just so you will know, many survivors report that the death has brought new relationships into their lives that offer tremendous support and friendship. They may be other survivors, friends who have lived through a tragedy or loss of their own, or just kind and compassionate people who want to be of help.

Coping with the Enormous Pain

Listed below are ways that people cope with the sudden death of a loved one. We first list some of the healthier ways of coping that survivors have developed.

Healthy Coping Behaviors:

Talking with someone who is a good listener
Talking with your departed loved one
Visiting the grave
Crying
Sleeping with or wearing the clothing of your loved one
Reading books related to your loss
Joining a support group and sharing your story with people who
    have been through similar experiences
Keeping a journal of feelings and reactions
Visiting a helpful Internet site
Getting exercise appropriate to your age and physical condition
Developing a plan to remember and honor your loved one, such
    as creating a memorial fund or organizing a tree planting
Finding soothing activities such as going for a walk in the woods
    or taking a long bath
Creating a photograph album or memory book
Finding a grief counselor

Unhealthy Coping Behaviors:

There are also unhealthy and maladaptive ways of coping with the pain. Some of them are okay when used in moderation, but become problematic when used in excess to constantly escape the reality of the death.

Using work as an escape
Taking excessive time off from work
Using sleep as an escape
Constantly reading books or watching television as a distraction

Other behaviors are clearly self-destructive and likely to cause more harm than good;

Anger reactions: behaviors that physically or emotionally hurt another person, such as yelling, screaming, and becoming physically abusive. It's okay to be angry, but do not get to a point where you become hurtful to yourself or someone else.

Extreme denial reactions: constantly pretending to yourself or others that your loved one is still alive, not mentioning your loved one's name again, trying to erase the memory of your loved one.

Escape through: use of alcohol, drugs, over- or under eating, compulsive sexual behavior, gambling, or overspending.

Suicidality: Sometimes the pain of loss becomes so intense that survivors contemplate taking their own lives. If these feelings persist or seem to be growing over time, we urge you to confide in a trusted friend or doctor, and to seek help from a mental health professional. Please do not make the mistake that your loved one made. Your life matters, and your friends and family would be devastated by losing you, just as you have been devastated by the loss of your loved one.

Feeling (or Not Feeling) the Presence of Your Loved One

If you have a difficult time bringing to mind the face of your loved one, it might be helpful to look at pictures or videos and to tell stories about the person's life. If you presently find this too painful, give yourself time to ease into the pictures and stories. Some people report that they feel the presence of their loved one after the death. Some feel it constantly while others feel it only once in a while. Other people report dreams, visions, sounds, or tactile sensations that convince them that they are in the presence of their loved one. These reports are not unusual, and your task is to decide what the experiences mean for you. If you are concerned about these events, talk to a counselor knowledgeable about grief. Survivors who have not had such experiences sometimes wonder why they have been "left out," perceiving it as a further rejection from their loved one. It is not clear why some people have these experiences and others do not, and we would not presume to try to explain this phenomenon. We can tell you that while most survivors do not report such experiences, a significant minority does. The presence or absence of seemingly supernatural experiences is not a measure of the love you had for your loved one, or your loved one for you.

Re-traumatization and Grief

You may learn about a suicide similar to your loved one's on the news, on a television or movie drama, or simply from other people. Suddenly you may find yourself reliving the events surrounding your loss and empathizing with the family in the story. There is a term for these strong, unexpected reactions: grief attacks. Consider taking a break from news reports or violent movies. And be patient with yourself. The fact is, years later grief reactions can still emerge. Fortunately, survivors learn to manage these emotional episodes more easily as time goes by.

Taking Care of Yourself

Even though you may not feel like it, we urge you to do things that will keep yourself healthy. Your body and your spirit have been wounded by this loss, and you must make an extra effort to care for both. To help your body recover, it is crucial that you eat healthy food, get sufficient rest, exercise in moderation, and be careful about alcohol and drug usage. To help heal your spirit, find activities that bring a sense of comfort and emotional nourishment, such as writing, listening to music, going for walks, and talking with friends who will not judge you.

THE FIRST YEAR AND BEYOND

The One Year Date

Many people view the one-year date of the death as an important milestone, and indeed it is. You have made it through a year's worth of holidays, birthdays, and just ordinary days of missing your loved one. While it sometimes seems as if the suicide was long ago, it also can feel like it just happened. While you have come out of the fog you were in right after the death, at times the pain can still seem unbearable. As you approach the one-year date, you may find yourself experiencing an upsurge of grief, including some of the reactions that you experienced early in the mourning process. You may also find yourself in a kind of mental countdown, vividly remembering the days that preceded the death of your loved one. All of this is sometimes referred to as an "anniversary reaction." It is quite normal. While many people dread the day, most people find that the anticipation is often worse than the actual day itself. It will probably help if you plan carefully how you want to spend the day. Are there people in your life (for example, at work) whom you should remind about the one-year date, so that they can understand what you are going through? Do you want to be alone or with people? Which people? Do you want to keep your usual routine or do you want to take the day off? How do you want to mark the day? Many people find that some sort of ritual that memorializes and honors their loved one is very comforting (see **Holidays and Other Important Dates** on page 40). If you plan ahead for the day, it will probably be easier for you to move through it.

Some survivors have unrealistic expectations for the one-year date. People around you may assume that once you have passed a year, you will be "over" your grief. You may have harbored this expectation yourself. In all likelihood, you are now discovering that this is not the case. If your grief continues, then you are experiencing the norm. While passing the one-year mark does prove that you are a survivor, there is nothing magical about 365 days. Your loved one will still be gone on day 366, and the hole in your life will still be there. You will still have periods when you miss your loved one intensely and the world seems out of order. As we have tried to stress, grieving is a "two steps forward, one step back" kind of experience. Perhaps it is more like learning to live with a permanent injury than getting over, say, the flu. You will need to be patient with and protective of yourself as you go on from here.

Depression

As the months go by, you may feel yourself slipping into a state of confusion, anger, and dejection. You may feel worthless, that life has no purpose, or perhaps worry that you are going crazy. You may feel fatigued much of the time. You may not be fully functioning at work or in the family. Your sleep may still be poor, and you may have early morning awakening, unable to return to sleep. You may even be entertaining your own thoughts of suicide. Perhaps these problems have steadily worsened since the suicide.

All of these feelings suggest that your grief may be hardening into what mental health professionals call a clinical depression. Early on in grief, it is virtually impossible to distinguish between grief and depression. But for some people, a serious loss can trigger a depression that requires help from a competent mental health professional. If it is more than a year since the death and the quality and intensity of your grief has changed very little or is getting worse -- and certainly if you are feeling suicidal -- then it is time to seek out an experienced therapist (a psychiatrist, psychologist, social worker, or other mental health professional). This person should be able to help you sort out your feelings and decide what type of counseling and/or medication might be beneficial. Try to find someone who understands both the phenomenon of clinical depression and the grieving process after suicide. Unfortunately, not all mental health professionals do.

Support Groups

You are not alone in your hardship and grief. Sadly, each year in the U.S., more than 30,000 people take their lives. Many other people have also experienced the suicide of a loved one (a conservative estimate is that somewhere between 4 and 5 million Americans have lost someone close to them to suicide). Some have transformed their tragedy into a mission to help those touched by suicide. They are committed to be there for you as you search for elusive answers. They are there to listen to and support you. There are bereavement support groups across the United States to help survivors. These groups are often organized by people who, like yourself, have had a loved one die from suicide, or by mental health professionals experienced at working with survivors. When you walk into your first meeting, you will see the faces of people who know the pain of this type of traumatic death. You may meet survivors of one month, one year, or ten years. They will listen to your story, share their own, and offer help where they can. They are ready to reach out to you and your family for however long you desire. Many survivors who have attended a support group report that they received hope, comfort, friendship, and compassion —support that may have literally saved their lives. Call your local crisis center or mental health clinic.

You can also contact:

The American Association of Suicidology (202) 237-2280, web site: http://www.suicidology.org or
The American Foundation for Suicide Prevention (888) 333-2377, web site: http://www.afsp.org.

Both organizations maintain lists of survivor support groups around the United States. (Our resource list, which begins on page 57, provides additional suggestions.)

Deciding to Go to a Support Group Meeting

Going to a support group meeting may be a hard decision for you to make. You didn't ask for this tragedy in your life. You may wonder, "Why do I need to attend a meeting with grieving people I don't even know?" You may come up with all sorts of reasons why you should not sit in on such a group. But if you take the step to try a grief support group, you may find that this is the only place you will be able to talk openly about your feelings, your loved one, and the impact of the suicide on your life. One suggestion: after you have attended your first meeting: do not decide about returning until you have attended a second or third. And be ready to awaken the next day with, as some people describe it, an "emotional hangover," because you have done some hard but necessary work.

Other Bereavement Resources

There are self-care books written by people who have experienced the suicide of a loved one and by mental health professionals with extensive experience with survivors. See Appendix on page 57 for suggested readings. In addition, there are books that can help you understand some of your grief reactions and those of your children. Books on more specific topics -- such as the death of a spouse, sibling, child, parent, or other loved one -- are also available. You will find some of these volumes at your local bookstore or library; and bookstores can order any book in print for you. Some cities also have support groups especially designed for children and for adolescents coping with a death.

Holidays and Other Important Dates

It will be helpful if you and your family seek ways to face the holidays and other important dates (such as birthdays and anniversaries) because there will be other family members (children and grandchildren) who will need you. Here are some suggestions for coping with these difficult days from people whose loved one has died:

Send off balloons.
Set a place at the table for your loved one.
Light a special candle.
Tell stories of the person.
Sing or listen to a special song.
Create an ornament to hang on a tree or a wall.
Visit a special place that is associated with your loved one.
Write a letter to your loved one. Consider reading it to
    someone else.
Create a web site to honor your loved one.
Buy your loved one a present.
Make your loved one's favorite meal or dessert.
Plant a tree, a bush, a flower.
Say a special prayer.
Make a quilt with the clothing of your loved one.
Change old traditions and begin new ones.

Life after Suicide

We have seen people walk into a support group meeting emotionally crippled because their loved one died from suicide. We have known people who could never imagine laughing again. We have held in our arms people who have sobbed helplessly because they felt they could never have a future without their loved one in their life. But in time, we have seen these same people move from deep despair to a new life. Please don't misunderstand us. These survivors will never forget their loved one. They carry this person in their heart. Their grieving continues to ebb and flow as the years go by. They still experience the "grief attacks" noted earlier.

With a good network of support, you may find that you tap into depths of character beyond your comprehension. You are a survivor of the suicide of a loved one. Even when you find yourself believing that you cannot bear the sorrow any more, you must believe that you can take another step to make it through one more day. Try to figure out ways to get yourself and your family through this maze of grief. Believe that you can survive even when you are convinced that you are sinking. Do not avoid your grief -- talk about it until you are on top of it. Others have survived this type of tragedy and you can, too.

Be patient and kind with yourself. Recognize progress in your grief when it occurs. When your loss is not the first thing you think about when you wake up, that's progress. When the death, the suicide, and your grief are not the last things you think about before falling asleep, that is progress. When you notice that there are longer periods of time when you are not thinking about the pain you have been through, that is also progress. Don't be frightened by these shifts. Progress does not mean that you are forgetting your loved one. You will always carry him or her in your memory and in your heart. Over time, you will also begin to realize that suicide was only a part of your loved one's life story. He or she also had moments of joy, humor, love, and achievement. When you can remember and savor all of these memories, you will know that you are making progress.

Your View of the World Has Changed

When a tragedy occurs, your view of the world may suddenly and permanently change. It is as if an earthquake has destroyed part of the structure of your life. A suicide can undermine your sense of trust in others, and your belief in your own competence, self-worth, and mastery over your life. After such a tragedy, the universe itself may no longer seem benevolent. A central task for you as a survivor of suicide is to rebuild your sense of safety, control, order, and goodness in the world. Like the survivor of an earthquake, you must decide whether to rebuild the structure of your life as it was before, whether to modify and strengthen it, or even whether to rebuild it somewhere else. For some, suicide produces a crisis of faith ("How could God let this happen?"). For others, it raises profound questions about life, death, and the purpose of living ("What do I believe about life after death? What is the point of my life?"). For almost all survivors, it produces a sense of having been injured by life, a realization that others whom you love can nonetheless do things that break your heart and wound your soul.

Yet unlikely as it may seem, we have also witnessed the struggle to cope with a loved one's suicide produce dramatic psychological and spiritual growth in survivors. Some individuals report that, over time, they have noticed positive changes in their outlook on life. They have come to understand that life is precious and without guarantees. They have learned "not to sweat the small stuff." Their values and priorities have shifted. Some feel a deeper sense of connection to something larger than themselves, whether it takes the form of God, or life, or their fellow human beings. Many vow not to put off important activities, such as visiting loved ones and expressing their love to others. Because they understand what it means to feel confused, helpless, and alone, many survivors develop a more compassionate understanding of others' pain. Having brutally confronted the fact that some people choose to end their lives, many survivors have become clearer about their own reasons to go on living.

We are not suggesting that survivors welcome the suicide. We know that you will always miss your loved one, and to some extent the pain will always be there. But countless survivors have told us that they have found ways to cope with and even grow from this terrible loss. In the next section, **Stories of Survivors**, you will see evidence of this change. Hold on to your hope for the future, when the pain will ease and wisdom will grow. Realize that a survivor is just that: someone who has managed to survive and grow stronger after the suicide of a loved one. We wish you our best as you travel the difficult journey of a suicide survivor.

STORIES OF SURVIVORS

We asked several survivors to share the story of the suicide of their loved one, what helped them the most as they struggled with their grief, and what advice they would offer to new survivors. We thank these brave folks for caring enough to bare their souls, in the hope that it may show that you are not alone.

Peggy Anderson

My husband, Dave, was only 44 when he died from suicide. He rode his bicycle several miles to the Aurora Bridge, chained it up, and jumped to the water below. It was a beautiful Sunday morning in May, 1998. It was a total shock to us all. No one had a clue that he would do something like this. He was the nicest guy in the world: friendly, outgoing, loving, cheerful, and playful. He was the greatest dad our daughter could ever have had. He was a wonderful husband.

I gathered all the strength I had and proceeded with living each day the best I could by relying on the love and the friendship of my family, friends, neighbors, community, and co-workers. The day after Dave died my boss brought in a counselor for my co-workers. When people I meet ask if I've been married, I say, "Yes, but I lost my husband three years ago." And when they say, "Oh, you're so young. How did it happen?" I say it openly that he took his own life. People see that I'm willing to talk about it and because I'm comfortable, so are they. I guess the fact that I'm not afraid or embarrassed to bring it up has made it easier for those around me to be of support. I don't keep it inside. I tell people what I feel and they support me. I have come to realize that you don't get over your grief; you just get to a different phase. My best friend has been there for me. On each anniversary of Dave's death she has given me card and a note. People also help me by bringing up Dave in conversation. For example, my sister sometimes says, "I wish Dave were here." It feels great to hear people say his name.

Kathy Melsness

My seventeen year-old daughter, Marlene, took her life in February, 1987, by sitting in her car in our garage with the motor running. She was a girl who acted as if all was well and hated to see others sad or upset. Her friends said that she lived more in the 17 years than most people live in a normal life. But she forgot to take care of herself after she had a good friend move away, a boyfriend drop her, a weight gain, and a drinking problem (which only later did I found out about). I was the one who found her with the engine still running and the car radio on. The next few hours and weeks were a blur of police, onlookers, my ex-husband, family members, the funeral with hundreds of mourners, and co-workers who held me when I cried at work and gave me a big teddy bear to hug when times got tough. One friend who was particularly helpful was Sue, whose own daughter had died from suicide a few years earlier. Later I figured out that Marlene had introduced me to Sue, probably knowing whom I should be with after her death.

Several months later I joined a grief support group for all kinds of child deaths. The sharing and listening to others, who had been through this, helped me to deal with Marlene's death, but didn't explain why. At work my fellow workers came up to share their stories of their loved ones who died by suicide. The local grade schools contacted me to attend "at risk" sessions and it was here that I began to share Marlene's story with the kids. After our talk they trusted me. Some of their stories were horrifying. Some of these grade school kids had attempted suicide at their young age! I have spoken to Washington state legislators on the need for suicide prevention funding. Joining the support group and getting to a place in my life where I can reach out, help others, and make a difference have all helped me cope with the death of my daughter. But I miss her everyday.

Colleen Ryan Prosser

Ryan Michael Vego, my only son, a handsome 32 year-old man, chose to end his life on St. Patrick's Day, 2000. He had extraordinary talents in art and music. Our family's heritage is Irish Catholic and he was proud of that. But his ancestors passed along something else: alcoholism. He was a binge drinker, and in spite of long periods of sobriety, the disease was relentless. There is no way to describe the feeling you get when you open the door to find a sheriff's chaplain standing on your porch. Ryan had hung himself on a bluff overlooking Puget Sound. At that moment my world changed forever.

What helped were the friends and relatives who came to the funeral home and memorial service who told stories about my son that touched me and made me laugh. People wrote notes to Ryan and posted them on the bulletin board. I treasure each of them. When my priest rejected me, I found another priest who immediately made room on his busy calendar. We met for several hours and he told me the church no longer considers suicide to be a mortal sin. Our physician, a thoughtful and sensitive man, prescribed antidepressants and medication to help me sleep. He also prescribed a 32-hour workweek.

As I looked for a way to deal with my incredible emotional pain, the thought of making it through an entire day was sometimes more than I could bear. So I'd think to myself, "I can make it through an hour, I can make it through the morning." Occasionally, it got down to making it through the next minute. I was lost. I read every book that I could get my hands on about suicide. I desperately wanted to be with my son. I came close to understanding the severe depression Ryan must have felt. I sought out grief counselors, but found not one who understood the trauma of suicide and the devastation and anguish felt by those left behind. That's when I called the Crisis Clinic and learned about the Survivors of Suicide group. My husband and I and Ryan's girlfriend, Heather, dragged ourselves to a meeting A ritual of the meeting is to open by introducing ourselves and telling who we'd lost, when, and how. What I heard astounded me. Finally! I thought. "Here are kindred spirits! Here are people who understand." I met people who had lost loved ones to suicide six months ago, a year ago, five years ago -- and look! They are still living! There is an end to the darkness. We cried and we laughed together. The group gave me comfort, practical ideas, support, love, and above all—HOPE! I feel I am a survivor and I've made a decision: the noblest tribute I can offer my son is to live my life to the fullest, and in the very best way possible.

Heather Allyson Dwyer

My boyfriend, Ryan Vego took his life on a cliff overlooking Puget Sound on March 17, 2000. Ryan and I met in Art school. During one class session he came to my defense when a teacher was criticizing me. He won my heart that day. We lost touch for a number of years and later reconnected as a couple. We both wanted children and developed a plan for a family. I knew suicide was an option for Ryan. I thought acknowledging the idea was enough. It wasn't. I was sent into a numbing shock when Ryan's stepfather called to tell me Ryan's body had been found. I never imagined that suicide would come to seem possible for me, too. After the shock lifted, Ryan's death took me to a place I had never been before -- a place inside me that I cannot find the words to describe. I was truly depressed and needed help before I hurt myself.

Ryan's mom, Colleen, asked me if I would like to join her for a Survivor of Suicide (SOS) meeting. I asked her to check it out and let me know if it was just a bunch of melodramatic people crying for a couple of hours. I didn't want to be told I didn't hurt as much because I wasn't a sibling, spouse, or parent. I was already seeing a therapist and it seemed like a lot of "grief work," as therapists call it, to add to my busy life keeping myself together at work and crashing into sorrow at home. I have been attending the SOS meetings for a year and have found that sharing my grief has helped me the most.

I have learned about grief, my emotions, my past, and my future. As the last one to see Ryan alive, I spent a year with tremendous guilt. One night at the meeting I learned a powerful lesson. Ryan had told me after many dark nights that I had saved his life. I learned that I do not have the power to save a life and I also do not have the power to make someone die. Such a simple idea changed my whole understanding of my life and of Ryan's death.

Right after Ryan's death I could not eat or sleep -- I was obsessed with thoughts about his death. I could not escape my pain. Now, with the grief work I have done during the past year, I am a stronger, more loving and better person because of Ryan's life. I feel Ryan is always by my side and this helps me navigate each day. I am a survivor.

<u>Jim and Pat Peta</u>

On September 13, 1994 our son James shot himself in the dining room of our home. After years as bedeviled detectives, we were forced to conclude we would never understand why. He was handsome, funny, and fun. He was not perfect. He was 17 years old. If he sent us signals of his intent through thought, word, or deed, we missed them. We are so sorry for his choice.

WE KNOW NOW:

This horrific tragedy IS survivable. There are 2,000 suicides a day worldwide, and many times that number left behind bewildered and broken.

As Survivors, we are not alone. Surviving this loss is a daunting journey: unpredictable and unstructured, without concrete linear stages or pre-determined timelines. We used all the resources we could find: a wise therapist, books, support groups, conferences, other Survivors.

Assimilating this loss into our lives in an ongoing process. We both grieve -- very differently. Everyone's grieving is unique to him or her. Some people will say you are going the wrong way when it is simply a way of your own. Sometimes the best answer to chaos is to just sit still. We have lost friends and rituals. We have made new friends and rituals.

We can say NO to people, places, events, and things that drain us of energy. We do not have to answer the phone. The machine can and will. Our energy is precious. Fatigue is not a friend. We acknowledge fragility.

James was a gift on loan to us. He was not our only blessing. We need to make a conscious effort to count those blessings-every day. Control is largely an illusion. A split second can change us forever. We need to take less for granted. We need to live in the moment we have.

We feel good in the company of other Survivors. Many begin this journey every day. We can help. Helping heals.

We have re-entered the world. We can love, laugh, and enjoy again. There is no quick fix for healing. There is no substitute for Time.

WE BELIEVE NOW:

We need to fight the Great Destroyer named Suicide on every front with our time, energy, and money. We need to throw our support to organizations and people that can help us do that. The work is not ours to finish, but neither are we free to take no part in it. We've met the Beast. In this Universe we share, we believe that James is safe, knows we miss him and that our love for him will never end.

Gerard E. Mahoney

The warm summer Saturday afternoon of August, 1997 is forever etched into my mind. My wife told me "your sister [AnneMarie] has called you three times from the Cape. She sounds upset but won't tell me what is going on." My worst fears were confirmed moments later when I spoke with my sister by phone: my 42 year-old brother David had ended his life. The daunting task of telling my parents that their son had hung himself at our family's summer home was left to me. That night was the beginning of my grief. It is a process that is still evolving. It now takes on a more positive tone as opposed to the painful, negative one it had back then in 1997. How? Maybe my answer is too simplistic: I try to channel the pain and agony into something positive for others and myself.

Fortunately, shortly after David's death my sister AnneMarie tracked down a bereavement counselor. My family was always one that kept things to ourselves. To think that we, my parents, sister, and I were going to sit down with a psychologist and talk about our family and David and his depression and his suicide.... to this day it is the wisest decision we ever made. It was through these sessions with Jack Jordan that we found out about AFSP, the American Foundation for Suicide Prevention and the wonderful programs they have available for survivors. This was the turning point in my grief.

Since David's death in 1997 I have reached out to some survivors, and when those conversations end I feel wonderful. I know I have helped somebody understand something about this awful hurdle many of us face in life. Perhaps I have pointed out to them a little tiny aspect of their loved one's life or death. Or maybe I have told them how I suffered anxiety and panic attacks some 14 months after David died and that it is okay, they will get through it. As I described recently in a talk I gave: "Survivors are those left behind who are charged with putting back the pieces of a puzzle that is often beyond solving."

The thing that helped me most with my grief is my faith. It is strong, and full of hope. My faith tells me my brother now rests in a place of peace and love. During the eulogy I delivered at David's funeral I spoke these words: "No more anguish, uncertainty or fear, peace at last." It is my hope and prayer that these words bring consolation to many survivors.

AnneMarie Mahoney

I will never forget the pain of that Saturday afternoon as long as I live. It was August 2, 1997. One couldn't have asked for a more perfect day to be on Cape Cod. My feet were dug into the warm powder-like sand as the afternoon sun beat down upon me. I could see from the corner of my eye two neighbors approaching. I rose from my chair to greet them and the expression on their faces told me something was very wrong. Before they said a word to me, I knew: "It's David isn't it?" I hadn't thought of anyone else: my husband, daughter or parents. I knew in my heart that it could only be my brother David.

Approaching the house, I saw numerous emergency vehicles lining the quiet street. The coroner's car was close by, confirming that he was gone. I felt a searing pain pierce my heart as I crumbled in my husband's arms. "Oh my God...David is dead." He had killed himself, and I wanted to die too. How would I get through this? Could I get through this?

The hours and days that followed were in some respects surreal. My parents had lost their son, my sister in law had lost her husband, and his children had lost their father. But... I had lost my brother. Who would know what I was feeling? Who could help me with my pain? I knew this was something that I could not get through on my own.

In September of 1997, I was fortunate to find a support group for suicide survivors. I remember that long ride home after the first meeting. Suddenly, a sense of peace had come over me as I thought about the others who shared their own stories of surviving suicide. I had something in common with each and every one of them. There were times that I thought perhaps I was ready to move on, but as each meeting approached, I was drawn back to the people that I had come to depend upon. I had found a place where it was safe to cry, share my thoughts and feelings, or just sit quietly.

As the fourth anniversary of David's suicide approaches, I have come to realize that it was only through the support of others who had experienced the same loss that I am now able to live more comfortably with the fact that I am a suicide survivor.

Trudy Sevier

My daughter Debbie died by suicide June 26, 1995. She was 27. She hung herself in the garage. I was out of state, as was her brother. The EMT's told my husband, who found her, that it was well-planned -- very much in character for Debbie. Debbie had made a suicide attempt 12 years before and had received extensive counseling at the time. We knew she was upset in 1995, but were unable to get her to accept help this time. We also believe she was anorexic, but this was never diagnosed.

My advice for others who must endure this tragedy is to take good care of yourselves. You did not choose the situation, but will have to deal with it for the rest of your lives. Find yourselves a support group. I have chosen The Compassionate Friends but there are others. I have sought counseling help and medication, but know that without the practical help from The Compassionate Friends, emotional survival would have been much more difficult. Also, seek out supportive friends who are not bereaved parents, and follow the rules of good health- eat right, get plenty of rest, exercise, fresh air, and spiritual refreshment regularly. Allow yourselves to be "pulled back into life" by family and friends. Taking enough time to grieve and figuring out how and when to rejoin life is a delicate balance and totally individual, but it is probably your most important task. As you go along, look for ways to reinvest and find enjoyment in life.

Jack and Mary Pat McMahon

On March 9, 1991, our son Matt shot himself in his bedroom. We were asleep in our room, awaking to a sound that has forever changed our lives. Matt was 23 years old and gifted with beauty and humor, intellectual talent and athletic ability: a golden child.

Shock and incredulity overwhelmed us. Suicide happened to other people. Somewhere, somehow, a huge mistake had occurred. The fragile fault line between other people and us had shifted. We had crossed into the shadowed world of suicide survivors. A world where we share our pain and sorrow, our love and laughter, our memories, joyous and bitter. Matt accompanies us on our journey. We hold him close. His smile flashes and sparks our souls with newfound abilities and strengths. We will love him forever. Our Matty.

Additional comments from Jack

I'm assuming you're reading this within days, weeks, or months of losing someone to suicide. I remember those first days, weeks, months with great clarity particularly the feelings of physical and mental exhaustion. I also remember feeling as though I was watching a movie from afar with me as the main character. These early days and weeks were the "zombie period". . . functioning like a robot and going through the daily activity of living without any joy or enthusiasm.

The anticipation of holidays, birthdays, anniversary dates were very difficult but the days leading up to the dreaded day were often far worse than the day itself. Take heart. With the help of family, friends, professionals and support groups, the pain will become much less intense. You'll be able to remember the good times. There will always be a piece of you missing but you will be able to achieve normalcy and some measure of contentment in your life.

Additional comments from Mary Pat

After all you've read there will be times that you think you won't or can't make it after the suicide of someone you love. If you can somehow remember the four words, "I can make it," you will. It has been ten years since the suicide of our son, Matt. The road is paved with pain and hurt, questions with no answers, silence on the part of many, old friends lost and new friends made. It's a long road -- difficult and oftentimes with the feeling of no progress. Sometimes, the measure of progress is not ours but that of well-intentioned friends. They "will" us to be done with our grief so they can be more comfortable with us. Do not be discouraged.

Seek help and comfort from other survivors or with a professional. For me, these were lifelines. Try to find a professional who works with suicide survivors or grieving people. There is no greater support than a group of your peers who have experienced the same loss. You will not be judged but understood and validated. These are the places where we can express our questions and anger, our overwhelming pain and bewilderment. No one can understand like someone who shares the same emotions. In a group, you too will eventually help someone else. Something you say will touch another. Be gentle to yourself. It is the time to lower the bar of expectation.

Will you ever forget the suicide? NEVER.
Will you be able to live with the suicide? YES.
Will this new life be happy again? IT CAN BE.

I wish you the ability to seek the help you need. I wish you loving memories of your loved one.

FOR THOSE WHO WISH TO SUPPORT A
SURVIVOR OF SUICIDE

This section is addressed to readers who wish to help a suicide survivor. When we asked suicide survivors how friends and family helped during the weeks and months after the death, here were some answers:

Learn about the wide variety of ways that survivors cope with a death by suicide.

Be a good listener—realize that while you can't fix grief, you can listen attentively.

Don't offer empty words of reassurance ("It'll be okay.") or clichés ("I know just how you feel."). The best gift you can give some one who is grieving is to realize that you <u>do not</u> know how he or she feels, but that you are open to being taught what this experience is like.

Tell survivors that you care — and show them.

Don't be afraid to say the name of the person who died, or tell stories about his or her life.

Allow the survivor to be in emotional pain. Don't look for a silver lining—there isn't one. Don't say things like, "At least he's out of pain."

Allow the survivor to cry and cry — or to shed no tears at all.

Be ready to hear, over and over, the story of the person who died; the circumstances of the death; and the current problems of the mourner.

As months go by, don't be afraid to ask, "How are you doing with _____'s death?" If the survivor answers your question, be prepared to simply listen. If the survivor would rather not talk about it at that time, respect the decision.

Remember the birthday and death day of the person who died and be sure to make a call or mail a card on those days.

Realize that each person grieves in his or her own way. Allow the person to feel whatever emotions arise. This includes guilt, anger, and sadness.

Find practical ways to help the survivor, such as offering to do errands, watching the kids, mowing the lawn, driving the survivor to an appointment, helping with chores, praying together, or simply sitting quietly with the survivor. Ask the survivor directly, "How can I help you?"

Watch for unhealthy coping behanviors (see pages 34-35) and suggest counseling, if needed. Otherwise, accept what may seem to you to be a prolonged period of intense grief reactions.

Don't set a timetable for the survivor to be "over it" or "back to normal." If the survivor seems to have an upsurge of grief even many years later, let the person know that this is usually quite normal.

Realize that the suicide has changed this person forever, and that the survivor may carry aspects of grief for the rest of his or her life. Suicide survivors will never be the people they used to be, but they can become stronger and more compassionate as a result of their tragedy.

APPENDICES

APPENDIX A

SURVIVING SUICIDE RESOURCE LIST

What follows are some readings and other resources that may help you cope with the suicide of your loved one. Try some out, and do not be discouraged if one reading or web site does not seem relevant to you. Survivors often have to try many different approaches before they find one that really speaks to their particular experience.

Suggested Readings:

Bolton, I. (1983). *My Son...My Son: A Guide to Healing After Death, Loss or Suicide.* Atlanta: Bolton Press. A personal account by a mother about the suicide of her son. A classic in the field.

Chance, S. (1992). *Stronger Than Death: When Suicide Touches Your Life.* NY: W.W.Norton. Written by a psychiatrist whose son died from suicide.

Colt, G. H. (1991). *The Enigma of Suicide.* NY: Summit Books. An excellent, although slightly outdated, summary of perspectives on the phenomena of suicide. Discusses biological, psychiatric, societal, historical, and cultural factors that may contribute to suicide.

Dunne, E. J., McIntosh, J. L., & Dunne-Maxim, K. (1987). *Suicide and Its Aftermath: Understanding and Counseling the Survivors.* NY: W.W. Norton. This book was written by and for professional counselors, but is easily understood by general readers. It remains a classic in the field of counseling suicide survivors.

Fine, C. (1997). *No Time to Say Good-Bye: Surviving the Suicide of a Loved One.* NY: Doubleday. Written by a wife whose husband ended his life.

Jamison, K. R. (1995). *An Unquiet Mind: A Memoir of Moods and Madness*. NY: Knopf. A superb autobiographical book written by a unique author. Kay Jamison is a psychiatrist, a world-renowned expert on bipolar disorder, and someone who suffers from the disorder and has made a suicide attempt herself. She provides a unique insight into the experience of psychiatric disorder and the suicidal mind.

Jamison, K. R. (1999). *Night Falls Fast: Understanding Suicide*. NY: Knopf. See note above about Kay Jamison. An excellent, very readable summary of what we know about the causes and prevention of suicide.

Lester, D. (1997). *Making Sense of Suicide: An In-Depth Look at Why People Kill Themselves*. Philadelphia: Charles Press. A summary of the research on suicide causes and prevention by a well-known suicidologist.

Marcus, E. (1996). *Why Suicide?* San Francisco: Harper San Francisco. A simple question and answer format that gives information about the causes of suicide.

Poussaint, A. F. & Alexander, A. (2000). *Lay My Burden Down: Unraveling Suicide and the Mental Health Crisis Among African-Americans*. Boston: Beacon Press. An important book, and one of the few about suicide and other mental health problems in the African-American community.

Rando, T. A. (1988). *How to Go On Living When Someone You Love Dies*. NY: Bantam Books. Though not specifically about suicide, this is an excellent book on grief that contains a chapter about suicide loss.

Ross, E.B. (1997). *Life After Suicide: A Ray of Hope for Those Left Behind*. NY: Plenum. An excellent book that emphasizes finding growth after the tragedy of suicide.

Slaby, A. & Garfinkel, L. (1994). *No One Saw My Pain: Why Teens Kill Themselves*. NY: W.W. Norton & Co. Written by an expert on suicide in young adults, this book explores many examples of adolescent suicide and the complex contributing factors.

Smolin, A. & Guinan, J. (1993). *Healing After the Suicide of a Loved One.* NY: Simon & Schuster. A useful guide by two therapists about coping with suicide, this book includes chapters on the loss of different relationships (spouse, child, parent, sibling, etc.).

Stimming, M. & Stimming, M. (1999). *Before Their Time: Adult Children's Experiences of Parental Suicide.* Philadelphia: Temple University Press. The first book devoted specifically to adults who have lost a parent to suicide as an adult.

Surviving Suicide. Newsletter published by the American Association of Suicidology. See below.

U.S. Public Health Service. (1999). *The Surgeon General's Call to Action to Prevent Suicide.* Washington, D.C. This landmark report issued by Surgeon General David Satcher enumerates the reasons why suicide should be considered a public health threat and outlines a plan of action to reduce suicide rates in the United States.

Organizations

American Association of Suicidology, 4201 Connecticut Ave. NW, Suite 408, Washington, D.C. 20008. Telephone (202) 237-2280. An organization of professionals dedicated to the study of the causes and prevention of suicide. AAS maintains a database of survivor groups around the country. (www.suicidology.org)

American Foundation for Suicide Prevention (AFSP) 120 Wall Street, 22nd Floor New York, New York 10005. Telephone (888) 333-2377. AFSP is a nonprofit foundation that supports research and education into the causes and prevention of suicide, and provides information and support to suicide survivors. AFSP maintains a database of survivor support groups, and runs an annual Survivors of Suicide teleconference in November, with viewing sites around the nation. (www.afsp.org)

Suicide Information & Education Centre (SIEC) #210, 1615 10th Avenue S.W., Calgary, Alberta, Canada T3C0J7. Telephone: (403) 245-3900. Largest database and library of information related to suicide in the world. (www.siec.ca)

Suicide Prevention Advocacy Network USA (SPAN USA) 4034 Odins Way, Marietta, GA, 30068. Telephone: (888) 649-1366. SPAN is a political advocacy group comprised of survivors, professionals, and political leaders. The mission of SPAN is to help reduce the suicide rate in the United States by advocating for suicide prevention programs aimed at the public, and at government and other social institutions. (www.spanusa.org)

APPENDIX **B**

SUICIDE AND PSYCHIATRIC ILLNESS

Throughout history, suicide has been attributed to many different causes: insanity; moral weakness, cowardice, impulsiveness and other character flaws, excess stress, social pressure, social rejection or loss, heroism (as in giving one's life for a noble cause), social disorganization and disruption, the devil, and a host of other explanations. While the causes of suicide are in many ways still a mystery, there is growing, scientifically based evidence that suicide is highly associated with, and in the majority of cases, the result of psychiatric disorders. Estimates are that up to 95% of all people who kill themselves are suffering from a diagnosable psychiatric disorder at the time of their death. This does not mean that the individual was "crazy", or even that they had been suffering from the disorder all of their life. Depression is the most common correlate of suicide. Other psychiatric disorders often associated with suicide are bipolar disorder, schizophrenia, and substance abuse. Medical research is also demonstrating that these major psychiatric disorders involve changes in the functioning of the brain that can severely alter the thinking, mood, and behavior of someone suffering from the disorder. This means that while stress, social problems, and other environmental factors can contribute to the development of a psychiatric disorder, the illness produces biological changes in the individual that create the emotional and physical pain (depression, inability to take pleasure in things, hopelessness, etc.) which contribute to almost all suicides.

Psychiatric disorders can be treated, and with good mental health care, most people can be helped to a full or at least partial recovery. Sadly, as with other illnesses, today's treatments are not yet good enough to help everyone. Equally important, because of the stigma connected with mental illness in our society, along with the widespread under-funding of mental health services, millions of people who could be helped either are reluctant to seek or are unable to find competent mental health treatment. We strongly encourage all survivors to educate themselves about mental illness and suicide. This will help you to better understand the illness that most likely contributed to your loved one's death, and perhaps empower you to combat the shame and ignorance that still surround psychiatric disorders in our nation.

For more information about psychiatric disorders, contact:

The National Institute of Mental Health (www.nimh.nih.gov), The American Foundation for Suicide Prevention (www.afsp.org), The American Psychiatric Association (www.psych.org) or the American Psychological Association (www.apa.org).

Appendix C

When to Seek Professional Help

Some suicide survivors include therapy with a mental health professional as part of their cooping process. Others often ask "How do I know when to seek outside help? How do I find a competent therapist?" We will try to briefly address these complex questions here. We want to begin by emphasizing how crucial it is to take care of your physical and your mental health in the aftermath of a suicide of a loved one. If you were severely injured in an automobile crash, you would expect to go through a period of convalescence, where you rested, paid extra attention to your body's functioning, and received professional "rehabilitation" help. It is no different when one has experienced an emotional "crash". You must pay attention to your mood, your thinking, and your behavior, monitoring them for warning signs that extra help may be in order. These warning signs can include: increased use of chemical substances to control the emotional pain; a persistent depressed mood that grows steadily worse over time, particularly if it includes hopelessness and thoughts of ending your own life; anxiety symptoms that significantly interfere with your functioning (e.g., difficulty leaving the house); excessive avoidance of people; intrusive flashbacks of your loved one's death and active avoidance of any reminders of the death; difficulty functioning at work or at home that does not improve with time; and extreme and persistent denial of the reality of the death. All of these symptoms can be common and normal in the beginning of the grieving process. However, if they persist or increase, rather than gradually decreasing over time, they are indications that a consultation with a mental health professional is appropriate.

Finding a knowledgeable and caring mental health professional is not always easy. Unfortunately, most training programs for such professionals do not include much instruction in dealing with bereavement let alone grief after suicide. A therapist should be someone with whom you feel trust, respect, and emotionally safe. Ideally, he or she should also be knowledgeable about grief, suicide, when it is appropriate to refer for medications, and about how to help with the specific problems that are troubling you (depression, anxiety, unending grief, etc.).

Please be aware that it is not only okay, but a good idea to "shop" for a therapist until you find one that you feel confident can be of help to you. Begin your search by checking with family and friends who may have seen a therapist, with your primary care physician, or with your local mental health center or hospital based psychiatry department. The state professional associations of psychiatrists, psychologists, marriage and family therapists, and social workers in your area will also likely offer a referral service (the professional discipline is less important the clinician's experience and your comfort level with them). Be sure to explain that you would like someone who specializes in working with bereavement. Finally, check with the Association for Death Education and Counseling (telephone (860) 586-7503 or web page: www.adec.org) for a referral to a grief counselor near you. Good luck, and do not give up until you find someone who provides the help that you need.

ACKNOWLEDGMENTS

We thank the following people for their valuable input in reading drafts of this booklet. We are sincerely grateful for their assistance.

Paige Alvord	Jack McMahon
Peggy Anderson	Mary Pat McMahon
David Breakstone	AnneMarie Mahoney
Ron Callahan	Gerard Mahoney
Lew Cox	Alicia Matthiesen
Carole Duncan	Kathryn Melsness
Heather Dwyer	Jim Peta
Sue Eastgard	Pat Peta
Laura Edwards	Colleen Ryan
Nancy Ekdahl	Trudy Sevier
Ruth Hargiss	Kristen Young
Jane Jackson	Mary Young

We would like to add a word of thanks to Ms. Madeline Drexler, who provided editorial assistance with the final draft of the booklet.

Thanks also to Bob's wife, Kris, for her computer, production, and design expertise in preparing this booklet for printing.

ABOUT THE AUTHORS

Bob Baugher is an Instructor in Psychology and Certified Death Educator at Highline Community College in Des Moines, Washington. Since 1977 he has taught a class entitled "Death and Life," and for the past five years he has been a suicide intervention trainer working with the Washington State Youth Suicide Prevention Program. As a bereavement counselor and group facilitator, Bob has helped people who have experienced the death of a child, sibling, spouse, parent, partner, and friend. In 2001 he was awarded Professional of the Year by The Compassionate Friends, a national support group for bereaved parents and siblings. During the past ten years, Bob has given more than 300 workshops on coping with grief and has written five other books.

Jack Jordan is a psychologist in private practice in the Boston, Massachusetts area. He is also the founder and Director of the Suicide Grief Support Program at the Trauma Center in Allston, Massachusetts. He has worked with survivors of suicide and other losses for more than 25 years. He has also published articles in professional journals about grief counseling and the unique bereavement experience of suicide survivors. Jack also provides training for counselors and therapists on grief counseling through the Sturbridge Group, a bereavement training and consultation collaborative (http://www.sturbridgegroup.com). Jack is an active member of the Board of Directors of the American Foundation for Suicide Prevention, New England Chapter.

DISCOUNTS FOR ORDERING MULTIPLE COPIES

2-10 copies	5% Discount
11-24 copies	10% Discount
25-49 copies	20% Discount
50-99 copies	30% Discount
100 or more	35% Discount

Price: $10.00 (U.S. funds) per copy
Add $1.50 postage for a single copy
Free postage for U.S. orders of 2 or more copies

Shipping: Canadian and out-of-U.S. orders will be billed according to postal rates.

Washington State residents add 8.8% sales tax.

Please allow 2-4 weeks for delivery.

Send Check or Money Order to:

*Bob Baugher, Ph.D.
7108 127th Place S. E.
Newcastle, WA 98056-1325*

OR

e-mail your order and you will be billed

b_kbaugher@yahoo.com

Other books by Dr. Bob Baugher:

- *A Guide for the Bereaved Survivor* with Marc Calija
- *A Guide to Understanding Guilt During Bereavement*
- *Death Turns Allie's Family Upside Down* with Linda Wong-Garl & Kristina J. Baugher.
- *Understanding Anger During Bereavement* with Carol Hankins & Dr. Gary Hankins
- *Coping with Traumatic Death: Homicide* with Lew Cox

Pricing and taxes subject to change without notice